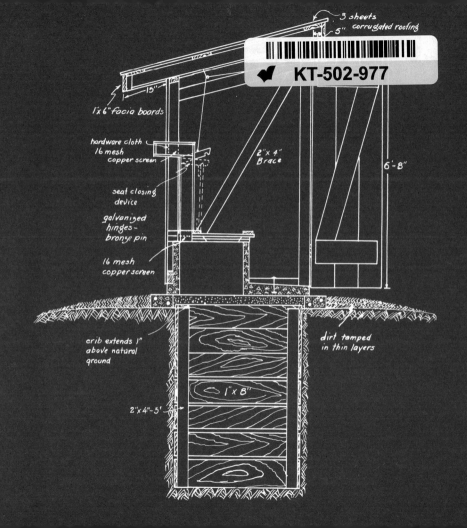

3 sheets
5" corrugated roofing

KT-502-977

15"

1"x 6" facia boards

hardware cloth
16 mesh
copper screen

2" x 4"
Brace

6'- 8"

seat closing
device

galvanized
hinges-
bronze pin

16 mesh
copper screen

crib extends 1"
above natural
ground

dirt tamped
in thin layers

1" x 8"

2"x 4"-5'

Ode to the Outhouse

A Tribute to a Vanishing American Icon

Foreword by Roger Welsch

With stories and artwork from
Charles "Chic" Sale, Bob Artley, and more

Voyageur Press

A TOWN SQUARE GIFTBOOK

Edited by Michael Dregni
Designed by JoDee Turner
Printed in Hong Kong

02   03   04   05   06   5   4   3   2

Library of Congress Cataloging-in-Publication Data
Ode to the outhouse : a tribute to a vanishing American icon / foreword by Roger Welsch; with stories and artwork from Charles "Chic" Sale, Bob Artley, and more.
        p. cm.
    "A Town Square Gift Book."
    ISBN 0-89658-598-0
    1. Outhouses—Humor. 2. American wit and humor. 3. Outhouses—United States.
I. Sale, Charles, 1885-1936.

  PN6231.O97 O34 2002
  818'.607—dc21
              2001057352

Distributed in Canada by Raincoast Books, 9050 Shaughnessy Street, Vancouver, B.C. V6P 6E5

Published by Voyageur Press, Inc.
123 North Second Street, P.O. Box 338, Stillwater, MN 55082 U.S.A.
651-430-2210, fax 651-430-2211
books@voyageurpress.com
www.voyageurpress.com

The Specialist by Charles Sale was reprinted by permission of Dwight and Laura Sale, the Specialist Publishing Company, 109 La Mesa Drive, Burlingame, CA 94010. *The Specialist* and its sequel, *I'll Tell You Why*, can be ordered from Specialist Publishing.

On the back cover: Painting the privy, 1962. (Photograph © Dave Hohman); **On the endpapers:** Privy plans from the Texas health department, circa 1930s. **On the frontispiece:** Dancing around the biffy. **On the title page:** A cowboy makes use of a Wild West nessy while his steed stands by. (Photograph © Londie G. Padelsky); **Inset on the title page:** A surfer visits the comfort station. (Photograph © Londie G. Padelsky)

Contents

HOLIDAY DECORATIONS
Christmas cheer comes to the biffy. (Photograph © Londie G. Padelsky)

A Note to All You Young Whippersnappers . . .

By Roger Welsch

Roger Welsch appears on CBS TV's Sunday Morning program, spreading the word about the glories of outhouses, old barns, farm living, and vintage tractors wherever the airwaves travel. His writings on vintage tractors appear regularly in Successful Farming *magazine's "Ageless Iron" section, as well as in* Esquire, Smithsonian, *and* Nebraska Farmer. *In addition, he is the author of more than twenty books, including* Old Tractors Never Die, *also published by* Voyageur Press.

PROUD PRIVY USER
Left: Roger Welsch models the latest in fashionable out-houses. (Photograph © Linda Welsch)

Right: OUTHOUSE ORIENTATION MAP

YOU ARE HERE

Go ahead and laugh. I know that's what you're here for. "Oh look at these pictures of quaint, even funny little buildings!" you're saying. "Can you imagine? People used to have a separate little buildings where they would go to poop! They'd walk out from the house maybe thirty feet or more, through the snow or heat, deal with wasps or snakes or skunks, and then relieve themselves right there *into* the ground! Gross! Yuk! Euwww! Ick. . . ."

Well, listen here, you young whippersnappers, if that's what you're thinking, you're dead wrong. Yes, there are people who used privies and hated them, and that's fine. There are men who wear suits and ties (Ick! Euwww!). There are women who tweeze their eyebrows (Gross! Yuk!). And frankly, I think people like me, people who consider the privy a lost joy, are a darn sight smarter than people who wear ties and tweeze.

It's easy to condemn something you don't understand. I have seen hundreds of museum visitors peer for a moment into a reproduction of a pioneer log cabin or sod house and comment on how small and dark and primitive it is, how much they who are oh-so-modern would hate

Nessy amidst the aspens
The autumn suns casts a golden halo over this privy in Inyo National Forest, California. (Photograph © Londie G. Padelsky)

AIR CONDITIONED
CABINS
FOR RENT!

BY THE DAY OR BY THE HOUR
KNEE ACTION WITH FLOATING POWER
OVER SIZED HOLES - TWO CATALOGUES
A NICE QUIET PLACE TO SIT AND THINK
RATES REASONABLE

Privy postcard, circa 1920s

to live there, how courageous the pioneers were to suffer through living in such hovels, aren't we lucky . . . and smart . . . to live in much, much nicer, much bigger houses. With patios.

Thing is, the frontier was huge, intimidating, and threatening. It was hard for a man to be out alone in his fields—gigantic compared to the miniscule fields and farms of the Old Country—alone, in constant danger; when he came home at night, he absolutely, most certainly did not want to sit outdoors on his patio in the wind and sun he'd been in all day. What he wanted was precisely what he built into his house—a dark, quiet, close, safe refuge. What's more, a shelter that he owned free and clear as opposed to the servitude he had been forced to suffer back across the ocean.

Those tiny, dark little frontier homes were not a burden on the pioneer soul; they were symbols of triumph and security.

Now, back to the outhouse. Believe it or not, there is a logic and comfort in the humble privy too, and there are still some of us who have used them, appreciated them, and, well, yes . . . it's true . . . miss them.

Not me. Yes, I have used them, and I appreciate them, but I don't miss them. I still have a couple around here on our farm.

Daughter Antonia won't use them . . . she's too young. Wife Linda won't use them . . . she's too delicate. Me, I use our outhouses, and one of the main reasons I use them is because the womenfolks don't use them. Two women in a house—have you ever lived in a situation like that? A man with two women in the house, even in urgency, might just as well get used to using a tree in the backyard for his, uh, necessities. Or more pleasantly, his outhouse.

My favorite outhouse, the one close to the house rather than down by my log house near the river, is old. I got it in 1974 and it was ancient then. I suspect it is close to a hundred years old by now, an architectural antique. I reshingled it, painted it, added a large picture window to the west over our farm's woodlands, built a sturdy shelf along one wall to hold the encyclopedia.

Yes, I have the requisite spicy girlie magazines and catalogs in my privy, but I consider my outhouse a place of opportunity as well as comfort, so I thought that I should now and again take a break from enjoying the beautiful scenery of the Middle Loup River Valley (or of Miss August for that matter) and flip open the Aa–Be volume, or perhaps Mf–Nu and learn what I could in those few otherwise idle moments. (It never for a moment bothered me that volume Lo–Me was missing from my privy encyclopedia, although I did occasionally wonder where it might have gone. It's not as if I could have misplaced it, after all.)

THE START OF PRIVY COLLECTING MANIA
James L. Johnson of West Unity, Ohio, is the author of the cartoon strip Horsecollars 'n' Pinfeathers. (Cartoon © James J. Johnson)

As a public service to cows . . .
Bossie scratches her head on a ranch privy. (Photograph © Londie G. Padelsky)

16

Embarrassment? When people understood such things, they put a wood pile near the outhouse. That way, if you were half way out there and realized the building was already in use, you could grab a couple sticks of firewood and return to the house as if that was your intent all along. Or if you absented yourself from company, you simply returned with an armload of wood a bit later. No explanation necessary.

The sun on my knees, my conscience clear, nary a moment's worry about the resonances of my totally natural physiological functions bothering anyone else in my household, and most certainly not that ever-troubling reality of the modern bathroom that here am I pooping—and there is my toothbrush, not four feet away. There has always been a sense of comfort for me in the honest and airy outhouse that I find nowhere else in life.

As for the elements others find troubling about a privy, frankly, I am baffled. Odor? On the Nebraska Plains there are constant zephyrs of fifty or sixty miles an hour that make your puny bathroom exhaust fan look like a young girl's sigh next to the engine of an F-16. Besides, if you know what you are doing, a light sprinkling of wood ashes into the pit, politely referred to as "flushing the privy," takes care of the problem quite nicely. The wasps and snakes, I find, don't bother me if I don't bother them. They seem to understand. And so do I. I watch the wasps building their nests and tending to their children, and find inspiration. The snakes enjoy the warmth of the sun quite as much as I do.

For a while a skunk lived under the wooden floor of our "Eleanor" privy. I would go in there, perhaps stomp the snow off my feet and establish myself and after a polite interval, he would poke his head out from the hole under the door and so much as say, "Howdy, old friend! Good to see you again." He never gave me any trouble and I always liked to think that for that brief moment he appreciated the human race as closer kin than most humans like to admit.

Perhaps I should explain the use above of the word "Eleanor." A privy is *not* a privy is *not* a privy . . . There are privies, and there are *privies*. All my privies have been gifts from good souls who simply could not bear seeing a venerable, well-loved old building simply discarded, and somehow I must broadcast my appreciation, even affection for them. So people give their outhouses to me. The gentleman who gave me our Eleanor asked me quietly one day while I was moving some other buildings from his ancestral farmlands if I would also be wanting to take . . . "the *private* place," our modern word "privy" after all being derived from "private." I could see by the look on his face and hear in the tone of his voice that he was *asking* me to take his "private place," and I said I most certainly would be honored.

"OUTWITTED BY COMMUNITY SANITATION"
The government led the war on sanitation in the 1930s with "modern approved sanitary privy" plans available to one and all. (Library of Congress)

19

And I was pleased to do that, not simply because of his obvious trust in me but also because this was the finest privy I'd ever seen in my life. I mean, this thing is downright elegant. It is of generous proportion, has boxed vents on two sides to insure generous ventilation, has a fine wooden box for paper, magazines, and other accoutrements, screened overhead vents, and is generally of superior construction.

An official historical architect took one look at my prize and declared, "She's an Eleanor. Rog, you have yourself a genine Depression-era Eleanor." As I understand it, one of the social programs of the Work Projects Administration, Civilian Conservation Corps, and other Depression-era rural improvement programs was to nudge farmers into acquiring or constructing for themselves privies meeting government specifications, as developed by official, trained, government outhouse engineers and architects.

Apocryphally, perhaps as a right-wing effort at slander, the buildings were instantly attributed to the do-gooder attitudes and activities of First Lady Eleanor Roosevelt and were labeled "Eleanors," almost certainly in scorn. As usual with such nefarious efforts, the plot

OUTHOUSE IN THE SNOW
An open door beckons those in need to this privy in the Sierra Nevada Mountains of California. (Photograph © Londie G. Padelsky)

backfired and Mrs. Roosevelt thus became eternally identified with one of the finest, most successful programs installed by any government anywhere in the world even unto these seventy years later. In my opinion, anyway.

The outhouse is an icon of American culture. The humble "private place" has generated great literature—who can forget Chic Sales's *The Specialist*, a model of brevity, wit, and truth for any aspiring writer? Greek Cynic philosopher Diogenes Laertes spoke of them more than two milleniums ago: "The sun too penetrates into privies but is not polluted by them."

Our history is shot through with outhouse references—the tale, for example, of George Washington's brother, who tipped over the family outhouse and then admitted the misdeed to their father, hoping he would garner the same kind of approval George had gotten from admitting his sin of cutting down the cherry tree. But the father instead applied a leather strap across the lad's bottom. When the boy recovered from his tears and asked why George had been praised for admitting he had cut down the tree while he had been beaten for pushing over the outhouse, even with an honest admission, the father explained, "Because I wasn't *in* the tree when George cut it down."

"FIRST NIGHT IN THE COUNTRY" POSTCARD, CIRCA 1930S

EXCUSE MY HASTE!
THIS AIN'T ALL WIND!
WILL WRITE LATER!

HUMOROUS POSTCARD, CIRCA 1930S

And our folklore—what old-timer's retelling of Halloween stories is complete without at least one outhouse tipping? I don't know how many times I've been told about the once-standard gag of "molassesing" the seats of the privy at a home where a barn dance was going on. The lost art of "molassesing" consisted of smearing molasses or anything similarly sticky on the privy seat so that who ever applied himself or herself would soon be yelling for help to get unstuck, thus providing some uncomfortable humor for the rest of the evening to the assembled crowd.

Or the "sweetening" of a "sour" privy by sprinkling kerosene down into the pit, the family elder later going out there and without thinking rapping the glowing embers of his pipe into the adjacent hole—and ending up thirty yards out in the pasture when the outhouse blows up. Standard punchlines for that narrative vary from "Must have been something I *et*" to "Sure glad I didn't let that one in the house."

Endless stories of dollar bills being dropped down the pit, the sad loser then seen tossing a twenty in after it because "I'm sure not going to down there just for a one dollar bill!" Think of the narrative lore we are missing by no longer having privies behind every house!

Or almost missing . . . Not two weeks ago two geniuses from my little hometown of Dannebrog, Nebraska, accidentally dropped a checkbook down the hole of a nearby park chemical potty—the like of which are not *nearly* as pleasant, efficient, romantic, or funny as a *real* outhouse. Instead of taking a stick and simply stirring the lost checkbook—perfectly worthless as it is, after all—these guys took that stick, wrapped it with toilet paper, lit it on fire, and stuck it down in the hole, thinking they would then be able to spot the lost checkbook and—ugh!—fish it out with that stick. One of the effects of losing our outhouses is that we have also lost a scientific awareness of methane, it would seem. Of course once that flaming paper hit the pool of methane at the bottom of that pit, the park outhouse blew up and sent these two guys flying back to town to change their clothes and talk with someone about the price of eyebrow transplants.

Another whiz kid hereabouts put a topless barrel under his outhouse to keep the sandy soil from caving into the pit. When the barrel filled up, local wags suggested that he would be able to provide a drain hole in the bottom of the barrel simply by aiming his deer rifle down through one of the holes and firing two or three rounds through the contents and through the bottom of the barrel. Observers say he only fired once before realizing his mistake.

Yes, there are still old-timers and even some of us younger coots who struggle with the notion that moving the privy indoors was all that great an idea and certainly not much of a contribution to civilization. Right now the base of the toilet in my bathroom is leaking. I'll call a plumber. He may show up sooner or later. Shouldn't cost much more than a couple hundred dollars to fix, I'd guess.

In the meanwhile, I think I'll stroll out past the hollyhocks to my outhouse, grab a volume of the encyclopedia, look out across the scenery, and lament the days of yore, when the land and man were one, and the processes of nature were accorded the small respect of a home of their own.

CHAPTER ONE

An Outhouse by Any Other Name: A Glossary of Privy Parlance

It seems only natural that throughout history we have created many a name for the "unmentionable" that was the common privy. Polite euphemism, humorous slang, and derogatory pun all have seen service in describing this delicate subject. Here's a handy glossary to privy parlance.

HAPPY FARMER, FINE PRIVY, 1951
The outhouse was typically set apart from the farmhouse, just as other outbuildings were on a farm. This farmer stands proudly beside his backhouse on a Minnesota farm. (Minnesota Historical Society)

Outhouse or **Backhouse**: As the privy was often set away from the house, it was commonly known as the **Outhouse**, just as working buildings on a farm other than the barn are termed "outbuildings." **Backhouse** also referred to its location out back.

Private Place or **Privy**: The outhouse was known among the more prudish as the **Private Place**. From this term came the common slang, **Privy**. The term **Biffy** is believed to be a downhome derivative of **Privy**.

Necessary House or **Nessy**: The name describes simply and succinctly the service the outhouse provided. **Nessy** was a shortened version of the term. **Chapel of Ease** and **Comfort Station** played on the privy's function. **Shithouse** was a crude but straightforward evocation of the outhouse's purpose.

Loo: This common name has a long heritage. **Loo** is a widely used English and American colloqualism for a privy, but is believed to originate from the old French warning call, "Gardez l'eau!"—"Watch out for the water!"—that was shouted out when dumping cooking slops or chamberpots from an upper-floor window into an open street sewer. Those days are thankfully gone, but the word lives on.

THE WOODPILE
"A trip to the woodpile" was often a polite euphemism for a visit to the privy. Many folk built their woodpile next to the outhouse so they could load up an armful of logs on the return trip. (Photograph © Londie G. Padelsky)

Latrine: *Latrina* was the Latin term for a toilet facility; the term was Anglicized as **Latrine**.

Uncle John or **Aunt Sue**: Polite euphemisms for the outhouse, as in "I'm going to visit Uncle John." Any relative's name could be used. The phrase could also double as caustic commentary on said relative's character. The **John** was likely a shortened version of the phrase **Uncle John**.

Woodpile or **Rosebush**: When in polite company, it was often preferable to say you were on your way to the woodpile or the rosebush instead of annoucing that the privy was your destination. The downside to this show of good manners was that you needed to return with an armload of wood or a bouquet of flowers.

Sears Booth: Chicago mail-order monolith Sears, Roebuck & Company was famous for its thick catalog that did double duty as toilet

JAKE
Outhouses were commonly called "Johns" as well as "Jakes." Another slang term of unknown derivation was "Dooley," which became a favorite in Australia. And some people simply announced they were "Going to see a man about a dog." (Photograph © Londie G. Padelsky)

paper in the privy; **Sears Booth** paid homage to the company's years of faithful service.

Reading Room or **Library**: With the Sears catalog handy, the privy was often dubbed the **Reading Room**. Many folk kept other reading material at hand—from books of trivia to volumes of the encyclopedia—so you could edify your mind while in the **Library**.

Throne Room: A fine descriptive phrase for the royal room where one sits in state on the throne. Naturally, this phrase may incorporate none-too-subtle commentary on the current ruler.

White House or **House of Parliament**: The otherwise unblemished name of the privy was sometimes taken in vain by disgruntled voters, who would announce their trip to the outhouse as "I'm going to send a letter to the White House." In Canada, messages were addressed to the **House of Parliament**.

SEARS BOOTH
In honor of Sears, Roebuck & Company and the thick mail-order catalogs it produced, biffies were jokingly called the "Sears Booth" as many folk spent extra time reading the pages they then used as toilet paper.

CAPITOL BUILDING
Seats of honor were provided for the president and secretary of state in this Oregon outhouse. (Photograph © Carolyn Fox)

Eleanor: During the Great Depression, President Franklin Delano Roosevelt's Work Projects Administration sought to offer jobs and promote rural sanitation by building outhouses. Three-man teams would spend some twenty hours erecting a privy; the WPA labor was free, but farm families paid for the materials at a cost of about $17 per outhouse. And these were glorious privies, with cast cement floors and fancy ventilation shafts. Many politicos saw the WPA outhouse project as a wasteful boondoggle, and as a dig against the president, scornfully took to calling the privies **Eleanors**. Some folk also termed them **Roosevelt Monuments**.

Chic Sale: Charles "Chic" Sale was a 1920s vaudeville actor and comedian who penned a book entitled *The Specialist* based on one of his stage routines about a carpenter named Lem Putt who specialized in building privies. In fact, the book struck such a chord with people that it worked its way into popular jargon: Some folk began calling an outhouse not a "Lem Putt" but a **Chic Sale**—to the author's everlasting consternation.

CHAPTER TWO

Privy Trivia

As we once made use of outhouses several times a day, they naturally became a big—if unremarkable—part of our lives. It was only natural, then, that folklore and humor grew to surround the mythical privy, much like the daisies or gooseberry bushes that blossomed around the real thing out back.

PAINTING THE NECESSARY HOUSE, 1962
Many a youth remembers hot summer days spent painting the family privy. It was just another task on a never-ending list of chores. (Photograph © Dave Hohman)

VETERAN DOOLEY
Above: Back in the days before toilet paper, folk were creative in finding items for wiping their derrières. Corncobs, leaves, grass, rags, newspaper, dress patterns, and mail-order catalogs were favorites. This ancient privy in the ghost town of Bannack, Montana, probably saw them all. (Photograph © Carolyn Fox)

MODERNIZED NESSY, CIRCA 1950S
Right: When Englishman Walter J. Alcock patented toilet paper in the 1880s, many a biffy was modernized with the addition of one of the new-fangled, state-of-the-art roll contraptions that held the perforated paper. This swank Wyoming privy even boasted electricity—once upon a time, that is. (Library of Congress)

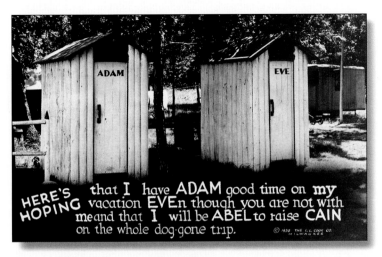

HERE'S HOPING that I have ADAM good time on my vacation EVEn though you are not with me and that I will be ABEL to raise CAIN on the whole dog-gone trip.

ADAM'S AND EVE'S, COMIC POSTCARD, 1938
Above: The sun—sol—symbolized man, and men's biffies often had a sun sawn in their doors. Folklorist Eric Sloane believed that in the late 1800s public places became less concerned with decorum, and men's outhouses went out of fashion due to the proximity of trees or bushes. Thus, only the privy with the crescent moon survived.

CRESCENT MOON
Left: Long ago, the moon—luna—symbolized womankind, and so some wag cleverly cut a moon into a privy door to advertise who was to use that outhouse, just like our modern-day signs for "Ladies" and "Gents." The crescent moon also provided light into the biffy—but it wasn't large enough for peeking toms, as a full moon might have been. (Photograph © Dennis Flaherty)

43

Two-stall nessy
Above: Before the days of indoor plumbing, almost all public buildings boasted an outhouse. Schools—such as this one-room country schoolhouse near Clay, Pennsylvania—as well as churches, stores, train depots, and government buildings all needed a nessy. Even the White House had a biffy. In fact, the White House had a telephone long before it had indoor plumbing. (Photograph © Keith Baum/BaumsAway)

Two-holer, circa 1930s
Left: Youngsters laugh today at the idea of communal two-holers, but once upon a time they served a real purpose. Most modern houses boast two and a half bathrooms, and so it should be no surprise that in the old days, families needed two—or more—holes in their outhouses. Often a third, smaller hole was provided for the children. (Library of Congress)

OUTHOUSE BEAUTIFUL
Above: Most biffies received only token interior decorating—usually just enough to make them pleasant during your brief visit. Currier & Ives engravings and other calendar scenes were often tacked up on the wall, but only the most swank jakes boasted painted interiors. (Photograph © Londie G. Padelsky)

ANY COLOR AS LONG AS IT'S WHITE
Right: Most thinking folk painted their privies white. Why? Simple. When the sun went down and you had to find your way to the necessary house after dark, the white paint aided navigation in the night. (Photograph © Carolyn Fox)

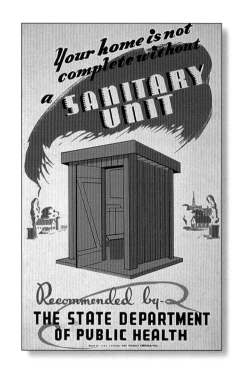

Sanitation is king, circa 1930s
From the days of the American Civil War, government public health departments made germs public enemy number one. While an understanding of how disease spread was still in its infancy, fear of typhoid, cholera, and other bacterial infections prompted government agencies to promote proper sanitation. (Library of Congress)

TEXAS COMMUNITY SANITATION HANDBOOK, CIRCA 1930S
Above left: Local health departments throughout North America issued plans such as these, advising folk on how to build their own sanitary privy.

PIT INSTRUCTIONS, CIRCA 1930S
Above right: Digging the privy pit was one of the few jobs where you started at the top and ended at the bottom.

49

COMFORT STATION
The memories of this former kid have not glossed over the past.

CHAPTER THREE

Memories of a Former Kid

By Bob Artley

Growing up on a farm in Iowa, the young Bob Artley was familiar with the privy and all the lore that surrounded it.

Artley not only had prowess squeezing milk from a cow's teat but could skillfully draw any bovine's likeness with a pencil and paper. He went on to study art formally at Grinnell College and the University of Iowa before becoming an editorial cartoonist first at the *Des Moines Tribune* and later at the *Worthington* (Minnesota) *Daily Globe* newspapers. Artley's long-lived series of autobiographical drawings "Memories of a Former Kid" is his masterpiece. He is also the author of *Once Upon a Farm* among books.

These reminiscences of outhouses past come from his "Memories of a Former Kid" series.

53

AFTER A WINTER STORM GETTING THE ESSENTIAL PATHS SHOVELED OUT AROUND THE FARMSTEAD HAD PRIORITY OVER **ALMOST** EVERY OTHER ACTIVITY.

57

Chapter Four

Bathroom Humor

There is a reason it was called "bathroom humor." Privy jokes once made prudish people politely titter while crude folk fell on the floor clutching their guts as they guffawed. Outhouse humor was common currency whether in the limelight of the vaudeville stage, around the cracker barrel at the general store, or while walking country lanes to school.

Comic postcards, circa 1930s and 1940s

Comic postcard, circa 1940s

PROGRESS

Outhouse calendar, 1953

Comic postcard, circa 1940s

HUMOROUS POSTCARD, CIRCA 1940s

Comic postcard, circa 1940s

Humorous postcard, circa 1940s

Humorous postcard, circa 1950s

HUMOROUS POSTCARD, CIRCA 1930S

HUMOROUS POSTCARD, CIRCA 1930S

Comic postcard, circa 1940s

THE SPECIALIST

BY CHARLES SALE

CHAPTER FIVE

The Specialist . . .
and a Brief Introduction to Outhouse Literature

By Charles Sale

In 1929, stage actor and comedian Charles "Chic" Sale of Urbana, Illinois, self-published a small book based on one of his vaudeville routines about a rural carpenter by the name of Lem Putt. The slim volume, titled The Specialist, *detailed Lem Putt's specialty: He was a champion architect, engineer, and constructor of outhouses. As Sale introduced his character,*

THE SPECIALIST
Published in 1929, Charles Sale's masterpiece of outhouse humor has sold more than two million copies worldwide. The Specialist *also inspired a whole field of literature devoted to privies—small books of folk humor and off-color jokes that tickled people's ribs from the 1920s through today.*

You've heerd a lot of pratin' and prattlin' about this bein' the age of specialization. I'm a carpenter by trade. At one time I could of built a house, barn, church or chicken coop. But I seen the need of a specialist in my line, so I studied her. I got her; she's mine. Gentlemen, you are face to face with the champion privy builder of Sangamon County.

Luke Harkins was my first customer. He heerd about me specializin' and decided to take a chance. I built fer him just the average eight family three holer. With that job my reputation was made, and since then I have devoted all my time and thought to that special line. Of course, when business is slack, I do do a bit paper-hangin' on the side. But my heart is just in privy buildin'. And when I finish a job, I ain't

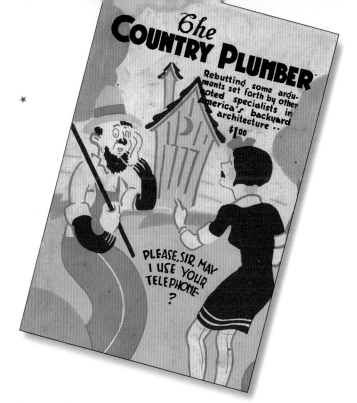

THE COUNTRY PLUMBER

Everyone knew privies were funny, but until the publication of The Specialist *no one realized how funny, as cash registers kept ringing up more sales. The Country Plumber of 1930 presented privy builder Phil Potts's rebuttal to Lem Putt.*

through. I give all my customers six months privy service free gratis. I explained this to Luke, and one day he calls me up and sez: "Lem, I wish you'd come out here; I'm havin' privy trouble."

So I gits in the car and drives out to Luke's place, and hid behind them Baldwins, where I could get a good view of the situation.

It was right in the middle of hayin' time, and them hired hands was goin' in there and stayin' anywheres from forty minutes to an hour. Think of that!

I sez: "Luke, you sure have got privy trouble." So I takes out my kit of tools and goes in to examine the structure.

First I looks at the catalogue hangin' there, thinkin' it might be that; but it wasn't even from a reckonized house. Then I looks at the seats proper and I see what the trouble was. I had made them holes too durn comfortable. So I gets out a scroll saw and cuts 'em square with hard edges. Then I go back and takes up my position as before— me here, the Baldwins here, and the privy there. And I watched them hired hands goin' in and out for nearly two hours; and not one of them was stayin' more than four minutes.

"Luke," I sez, "I've solved her." That's what comes of bein' a specialist, gentlemen.

'Twarn't long after I built that twin job for the school house, and then after that the biggest plant up to date—a eight holer. Elmer Ridgway was down and looked it over. And he come to me one day and sez: "Lem, I seen that eight hole job you done down there at the Corners, and it sure is a dandy; and figgerin' as how I'm goin' to build on the old Robinson property, I thought I'd ask you to kind of estimate on a job for me."

"You come to the right man, Elmer," I sez. "I'll be out as soon as I get the roof on the two-seater I'm puttin' up for the Sheriff."

Couple of days later I drives out to Elmer's place, gettin' there about dinner time. I knocks a couple of times on the door and I see they got a lot of folks to dinner, so not wishin' to disturb 'em, I just sneaks around to the side door and yells, "Hey, Elmer, here I am; where do you want that privy put?"

Elmer comes out and we get to talkin' about a good location. He was all fer puttin' her right alongside a jagged path runnin' by a big Northern Spy.

"I wouldn't do it, Elmer," I sez; "and I'll tell you why. In the first place, her bein' near a tree is bad. There ain't no sound in nature so disconcertin' as the sound of apples droppin' on th' roof. Then

THE RETURN OF LEM PUTT
The Specialist returned in the 1930 sequel "I'll Tell You Why" *with Lem Putt giving a pep talk to the Young Men's Business Breakfast Club on honor and ethics in the business of building outhouses.*

another thing, there's a crooked path runnin' by that tree and the soil there ain't adapted to absorbin' moisture. Durin' the rainy season she's likely to be slippery. Take your grandpappy—goin' out there is about the only recreation he gets. He'll go out some rainy night with his nighties flappin' around his legs, and like as not when you come out in the mornin' you'll find him prone in the mud, or maybe skidded off one of them curves and wound up in the corn crib. No, sir," I sez, "put her in a straight line with the house and, if it's all the same to you, have her go past the wood-pile. I'll tell you why.

"Take a woman, fer instance—out she goes. On the way back she'll gather five sticks of wood, and the average woman will make four or five trips a day. There's twenty sticks in the wood box without any trouble. On the other hand, take a timid woman, if she sees any men folks around, she's too bashful to go direct out, so she'll go to the wood-pile, pick up the wood, go back to the house and watch her chance. The average timid woman—especially a new hired girl—I've knowed to make as many as ten trips to the wood-pile before she goes in, regardless. On a good day you'll have your wood box filled by noon, and right there is a savin' of time.

"Now, about the diggin' of her. You can't be too careful about that," I sez; "dig her deep and dig her wide. It's a mighty sight better to have a little privy over a big hole than a big privy over a little hole. Another thing; when you dig her deep you've got her dug; and you ain't got that disconcertin' thought stealin' over you that sooner or later you'll have to dig again.

"And when it comes to construction," I sez, "I can give you joists or beams. Joists make a good job. Beams cost a bit more, but they're worth it. Beams, you might say, will last forever. 'Course, I could give you joists, but take your Aunt Emmy, she ain't gettin' a mite lighter. Some day she might be out there when them joists give way and there she'd be—catched. Another thing you've got to figger on, Elmer," I sez, "is that Odd Fellows picnic in the fall. Them boys is goin' to get in there in fours and sixes, singin' and drinkin', and the like, and I want to tell you there's nothin' breaks up an Odd Fellows picnic quicker than a diggin' party. Beams, I say, every time, and rest secure.

"And about her roof," I sez. "I can give you a lean-to type or a pitch roof. Pitch roofs cost a little more, but some of our best people has lean-tos. If it was fer myself, I'd have a lean-to, and I'll tell you why.

"A lean-to has two less corners fer the wasps to build their nests in; and on a hot August afternoon there ain't nothin so disconcertin' as a lot of wasps buzzin' 'round while you're settin' there doin' a little

HOLD EVERYTHING
Former Barnum circus clown Bob Sherwood offered this volume of musings on the dear old privy in 1929. The book was dedicated to the inventor of indoor plumbing.

readin', figgerin', or thinkin'. Another thing," I sez, "a lean-to gives you a high door. Take that son of yours, shootin' up like a weed; don't any of him seem to be turnin' under. If he was tryin' to get under a pitch roof door he'd crack his head everytime. Take a lean-to, Elmer; they ain't stylish, but they're practical.

"Now, about her furnishin's. I can give you a nail or hook for the catalogue, and besides, a box for cobs. You take your pa, for instance; he's of the old school and naturally he'd prefer the box; so put 'em both in, Elmer. Won't cost you a bit more for the box and keeps peace in the family. You can't teach an old dog new tricks," I sez.

"And as long as we're on furnishin's, I'll tell you about a technical point that was put to me the other day. The question was this: 'What is the life, or how long will the average mail order catalogue last, in just the plain, ordinary eight family three holer?' It stumped me for a spell; but this bein' a reasonable question I checked up, and found that by placin' the catalogue in there, say in January—when you get your new one—you should be into the harness section by June; but, of course, that ain't through apple time, and not countin' on too many city visitors, either.

"An' another thing—they've been puttin' so many of those stiff-coloured sheets in the catalogue here lately that it makes it hard to figger. Somethin' really ought to be done about this, and I've thought about takin' it up with Mr. Sears Roebuck hisself.

"As to the latch fer her, I can give you a spool and string, or a hook and eye. The cost of a spool and string is practically nothin', but they ain't positive in action. If somebody comes out and starts rattlin' the door, either the spool or the string is apt to give way, and there you are. But, with a hook and eye she's yours, you might say, for the whole afternoon, if you're so minded. Put on the hook and eye of the best quality 'cause there ain't nothin' that'll rack a man's nerves more than to be sittin' there ponderin', without a good, strong, substantial latch on the door." And he agreed with me.

"Now," I sez, "what about windows; some want 'em, some don't. They ain't so popular as they used to be. If it was me, Elmer, I'd say no windows; and I'll tell you why. Take, fer instance, somebody comin' out—maybe they're just in a hurry or maybe they waited too long. If the door don't open right away and you won't answer 'em, nine times out of ten they'll go 'round and 'round and look in the window, and you don't get the privacy you ought to.

The Passing of the Backhouse
Poet James Whitcomb Riley penned his poem in homage to the privy in the late 1800s.
No one knows for sure when it was written, as Riley was wont to hid his authorship of
the tribute in favor of his more serious poetry.

"Now, about ventilators, or the designs I cut in the doors. I can give you stars, diamonds, or crescents—there ain't much choice—all give good service. A lot of people like stars, because they throw a ragged shadder. Others like crescents 'cause they're graceful and simple. Last year we was cuttin' a lot of stars; but this year people are kinda quietin' down and runnin' more to crescents. I do cut twinin' hearts now and then for young married couples; and bunches of grapes for the newly rich. These last two designs come under the head of novelties and I don't very often suggest 'em, because it takes time and runs into money.

"I wouldn't take any snap judgment on her ventilators, Elmer," I sez, "because they've got a lot to do with the beauty of the structure. And don't over-do it, like Doc Turner did. He wanted stars and crescents both, against my better judgment, and now he's sorry. But it's too late; 'cause when I cut 'em, they're cut." And, gentlemen, you can get mighty tired, sittin' day after day lookin' at a ventilator that ain't to your likin'.

I never use knotty timber. All clean white pine—and I'll tell you why: You take a knot hole; if it doesn't fall out it will get pushed out; and if it comes in the door, nine times out of ten it will be too high to sit there and look out, and just the right height for some snooper to sneak around, peak in—and there you are—catched.

"Now," I sez, "how do you want that door to swing? Openin' in or out?" He said he didn't know. So I sez it should open in. This is the way it works out: "Place yourself in there. The door openin' in, say about forty-five degree. This gives you air and lets the sun beat in. Now, if you hear anybody comin', you can give it a quick shove with your foot and there you are. But if she swings out, where are you? You can't run the risk of havin' her open for air or sun, because if anyone comes, you can't get up off that seat, reach way around and grab 'er without gettin' caught, now can you?" He could see I was right.

So I built his door like all my doors, swingin' in, and, of course, facing east, to get the full benefit of th' sun. And I tell you, gentlemen, there ain't nothin' more restful than to get out there in the mornin', comfortably seated, with th' door about three-fourths open. The old sun, beatin' in on you, sort of relaxes a body—makes you feel m-i-g-h-t-y, m-i-g-h-t-y r-e-s-t-f-u-l.

"Now." I sez, "about the paintin' of her. What color do you want 'er, Elmer?" He said red. "Elmer," I sez, "I can paint her red, and red makes a beautiful job; or I can paint her a bright green, or any one of a half-dozen other colors, and they're all mighty pretty; but it ain't practical to use a single solid color, and I'll tell you why. She's too durn hard to see at night. You need contrast—just like they use on them railroad crossin' bars—so you can see 'em in the dark.

"If I was you, I'd paint her a bright red, with white trimmin's—just like your barn. Then she'll match up nice in the daytime, and you can spot 'er easy at night, when you ain't got much time to go scoutin' around.

"There's a lot of fine points to puttin' up a first-class privy that the average man don't think about. It's no job for an amachoor, take my word on it. There's a whole lot more to it than you can see by just takin' a few squints at your nabor's. Why, one of the worst tragedies around heer in years was because old man Clark's boys thought they knowed somethin' about this kind of work, and they didn't.

"Old man Clark—if he's a day he's ninety-seven—lives over there across the holler with his boys. Asked me to come over and estimate on their job. My price was too high; so they decided to do it themselves. And that's where the trouble begun.

"I was doin' a little paper hangin' at the time for that widder that lives down past the old creamery. As I'd drive by I could see the boys

REARS AND ROBUST

A take off on the Sears, Roebuck & Company mail-order catalog that provided toilet paper in many a biffy, the Rears and Robust book of the 1940s featured privy jokes printed on soft paper—including caricature images of Adolf Hitler for use on your backside.

a-workin'. Of course, I didn't want to butt in, so used to just holler at 'em on the way by and say, naborly like: 'Hey, boys, see you're doin a little buildin'.' You see, I didn't want to act like I was buttin' in on their work; but I knowed all the time they was going to have trouble with that privy. And they did. From all outside appearance it was a regulation job, but not being experienced along this line, they didn't anchor her.

"You see, I put a 4 by 4 that runs from the top right straight on down five foot into the ground. That's why you never see any of my jobs upset Hallowe'en night. They might *pull* 'em out, but they'll never upset 'em.

"Here's what happened: They didn' anchor theirs, and they painted it solid red—two bad mistakes.

"Hallowe'en night came along, darker than pitch. Old man Clark was out in there. Some of them devilish nabor boys was out for no good, and they upset 'er with the old man in it.

"Of course, the old man got to callin' and his boys heard the noise. One of 'em sez: 'What's the racket? Somebody must be at the chickens.' So they took the lantern, started out to the chicken shed. They didn't find anything wrong there, and they started back to the house. Then they heerd the dog bark, and one of his boys sez: 'Sounds like that barkin' is over towards the privy.' It bein' painted red, they couldn't see she was upset, so they started over there.

"In the meantime the old man had gotten so confused that he started to crawl out through the hole, yellin' for help all the time. The boys reckonized his voice and come runnin', but just as they got there he lost his holt and fell. After that they just *called*—didn't go near him. So you see what a tragedy that was; and they tell me he has been practically ostercized from society ever since.

Well, time passed, and I finally got Elmer's job done; and, gentlemen, everybody says that, next to my eight holer, it's the finest piece of construction work in the county.

Sometimes, when I get to feelin' blue and thinkin' I hitched my wagon to the wrong star, and may be I should have took up chiropracty or veternary, I just pack the little woman and the kids in the back of my car and start out, aimin' to fetch up at Elmer's place along about dusk.

When we gets to the top of the hill overlookin' his place, we stops. I slips the gear in mutual, and we jest sit there lookin' at that beautiful sight. There sits that privy on that knoll near the wood-pile, painted red and white, mornin' glories growin' up over her and Mr. Sun bathin' her in a burst of yeller color as he drops back of them hills. You can hear the dog barkin' in the distance, bringin' the cows up fer milkin', and the slow squeak of Elmer's windmill pumpin' away day after day the same as me.

As I look at that beautiful picture of my work, I'm proud. I heaves a sigh of satisfaction, my eyes fill up and I sez to myself, "Folks are right when they say that next to my eight holer that's the finest piece of construction work I ever done. I know I done right in Specializin'; I'm sittin' on top of the world; and I hope that boy of mine who is growin' up like a weed keeps up the good work when I'm gone."

With one last look as we pulls away, I slips my arm around the Missus and I sez: "Nora, Elmer don't have to worry, he's a boy that's got hisself a privy, a m-i-g-h-t-y, m-i-g-h-t-y, p-r-e-t-t-y p-r-i-v-y."

CHAPTER SIX

Architectural Gems: Outlandish Outhouses and Preposterous Privies

Architecturally speaking, outhouses perfected the rule of form following function. While other styles of architecture have been studied—from cathedrals to skyscrapers—little due has been given to the biffy. Yet while many a privy may have been a simple architectural gem, few architects ever drafted blueprints to build one; most outhouses were the results of downhome folk carpentry at its best. Still, whether purposeful or fanciful in construction, all nessies have served the same purpose with a grace of their own. The following privies were certainly built by visionaries handy with a hammer.

TREE OUTHOUSE
A hollow tree stump was converted into this funky outhouse in Washington. (Photograph © Londie G. Padelsky)

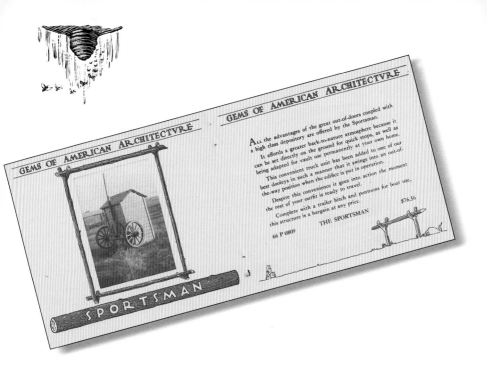

GEMS OF AMERICAN ARCHITECTURE

SPORTSMAN

GEMS OF AMERICAN ARCHITECTURE

ALL the advantages of the great out-of-doors coupled with a high class depository are offered by the Sportsman.

It affords a greater back-to-nature atmosphere because it can be set directly on the ground for quick stops, as well as being adapted for vault use permanently at your own home.

This convenient truck unit has been added to one of our best dooleys in such a manner that it swings into an out-of-the-way position when the edifice is put in operation.

Despite this convenience it goes into action the moment the rest of your outfit is ready to travel.

Complete with a trailer hitch and pontoons for boat use, this structure is a bargain at any price.

66 P 0809   THE SPORTSMAN $76.56

"GEMS OF AMERICAN ARCHITECTURE"
This little booklet—which purported to be a catalog of biffies for sale—was published as a promotional gift by Brown & Bigelow Advertising in St. Paul, Minnesota, in 1935.

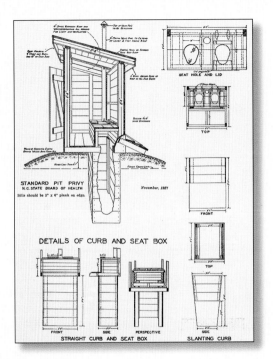

BIFFY BLUEPRINT

The North Carolina State Board of Health issued this blueprint advising homebuilders on how to construct the perfect two-hole nessy. All the details were here for the do-it-yourselfer—except advice on whether to cut a moon or sun into the door.

TWO-STORY PRIVY
Above: The idea of a second story on a privy made most people shudder. This double-decker still stands in the Nevada City ghost town in Montana. (Photograph © Londie G. Padelsky)

VICTORIAN OUTHOUSE
Left: Privy construction through time has included flights of whimsy such as this Victorian-style his-and-hers outhouse in Pennsylvania that was crowned by a cupola. (Photograph © Keith Baum/BaumsAway)

A-FRAME OUTHOUSE
Above: The sun shines beside the moon cut into this stylish A-frame privy in California. (Photograph © Londie G. Padelsky)

TENEMENT BACKHOUSES, CIRCA 1940S
Left: This double-stall, three-story outhouse was built onto a tenement building in St. Paul, Minnesota. Such sanitary services were common to many cities until indoor plumbing arrived. (Minnesota Historical Society)

There are flies upon the corncob
And slivers on the seat
But here's a childhood memory
That really can't be beat.

© C. T. & CO.

Chapter Seven

Sentimental Thoughts on a Vanishing Icon

It's a sad fact, but outhouses are a vanishing American icon. Indoor plumbing has put many a privy out of business whereas mobile plastic prefab biffies have taken the place of others. We leave you, then, with the following sentimental thoughts to bring back fond memories and a remembrance of things past.

SENTIMENTAL SENTIMENTS, CIRCA 1940S
Quaint poems of faux-mawkish nostalgia were popular comic privy postcards in the 1930s and 1940s.

PRIVY WITH A VIEW
(Photograph © Londie G. Padelsky)

100

You go here and I'll go there
We'll both be out of view
And while I sit in silent bliss
I'll think sweet thoughts of you!
© C. T. & CO.

THINKING SWEET THOUGHTS, CIRCA 1940S

The latch on the door
Is open to all
You furnish the corncob
We'll furnish the stall.

Above: WITH FOND REMEMBRANCE, CIRCA 1940S

OLD OUTHOUSE, FRESH SNOW
Right: (Photograph © Londie G. Padelsky)

The faithful outhouse amongst the autumn trees
Above: (Photograph © Londie G. Padelsky)

Come one, come all who seek relief
Perform the humble deed
Here beauty bows to duty
And pride makes way for need!

DUTY BEFORE BEAUTY, CIRCA 1940s

Comic postcard, circa 1930s

Ghost town privy at Bodie, California
Right: (Photograph © Londie G. Padelsky)

Overleaf: Forlorn and gray, circa 1930s

Here I stand
  Forlorn and gray
And my city cousin
  Gets a nickel a play.